CW00430694

IMAGES
of England

TORQUAY

William Kitson (1800-1883). The Local Board of Health was formed in 1850 to administer the affairs of the town. Kitson served as the first Chairman and his son, John, was the last. The Town Council replaced the Board in 1892 and, in recognition of the family's contribution to the town, John became the first Freeman of the Borough in 1909. William Kitson, a solicitor and banker with premises on Vaughan Parade, acted as land agent for the Palk estates and attracted the gentry to the Warberries and the Lincombes by leasing land to build mansions. Under his direction, the town became a fashionable watering place and he is now remembered as 'The Maker of Torquay'.

IMAGES
of England

TORQUAY

Compiled by
Mike Holgate

TEMPUS

First published 1998
Copyright © Mike Holgate, 1998

Tempus Publishing Limited
The Mill, Brimscombe Port,
Stroud, Gloucestershire, GL5 2QG

ISBN 0 7524 1165 9

Typesetting and origination by
Tempus Publishing Limited
Printed in Great Britain by
Bailey Print, Dursley, Gloucestershire

Other titles available from Tempus Publishing:

The Book of the Axe
Brixham
Around Exeter
Around Honiton
Around Ivybridge
Around Newton Abbot
Around Ottery St Mary
Paignton
Around Sidmouth
Tavistock
Teignmouth
Torpoint
Wartime Exeter and East Devon

Contents

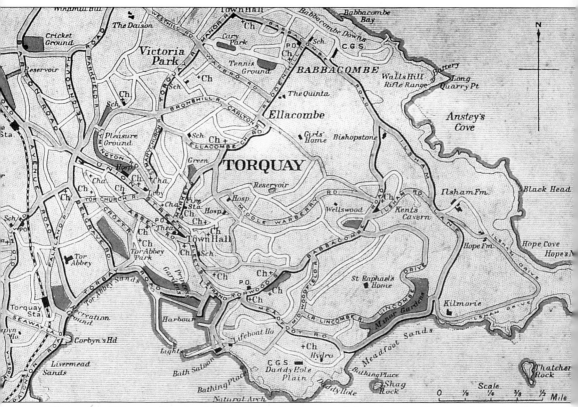

This map of Torquay appeared on an Edwardian postcard. It shows the Carnegie Library, which had opened at Castle Circus in 1907. On this map, the Town Hall is still situated in Abbey Road, as the present building was not constructed until 1911. Torbay Hospital and the Fire Brigade station, both later relocated on the Newton Road, are in Union Street and Market Street respectively, at this time. Some of the long-gone amenities represented on the map are Victoria Park and the Westhill and Walls Hill Rifle Range in Babbacombe.

Introduction

If 'every picture tells a story', a researcher would require the patience of Job and the imagination of Hans Christian Anderson to compile a book worthy of the vast pictorial archive held at Torquay Central Library's Local Studies Department. Many of the images donated are devoid of information regarding dates, events, and crucially, the identities of the people in the picture. That said, it has been my privilege to be allowed to select highlights from the many memorable occasions and slices of everyday life that this archive contains.

Some of the most stylish photographs of local life come from the work of James C. Dinham, a professional cameraman for over thirty years until his death at the age of fifty-one in 1912. A master of portraiture, he was favoured by Royal patronage and arranged sittings for many distinguished political and social figures including: Joseph Chamberlain, Winston Churchill, Jan Paderski and Dame Nellie Melba. His favourite subjects, however, were the great turn-of-the-century 'characters' found amongst the working-class street merchants and ragamuffins living in the poorer districts of his hometown. Examples from his unique *Torquay Celebrities* collection are featured throughout this book, on the opening page of each chapter – along with their original comic titles.

Mike Holgate
April 1998

Dinham & Sons, no. 34, Union Street. The premises have been decorated for a special occasion, possibly to celebrate the Armistice of 1918. The family traded at this address for fifty years, before the premises were taken over by jewellery chain, H. Samuel, in 1940.

J.C. Dinham was awarded a Royal Warrant in 1907, which continued to be held by his sons, Frederick and Edmund. Their photographs of royalty, including several of King George V and Queen Mary, are proudly presented in this 1922 window display.

One
Early Days

Raising the wind: 'Ome Sweet 'Ome', by J.C. Dinham.
The growth of Tor Quay, from a small fishing hamlet at the close of the eighteenth century into the home of 35,000 townspeople by 1900, is certainly something to trumpet about!

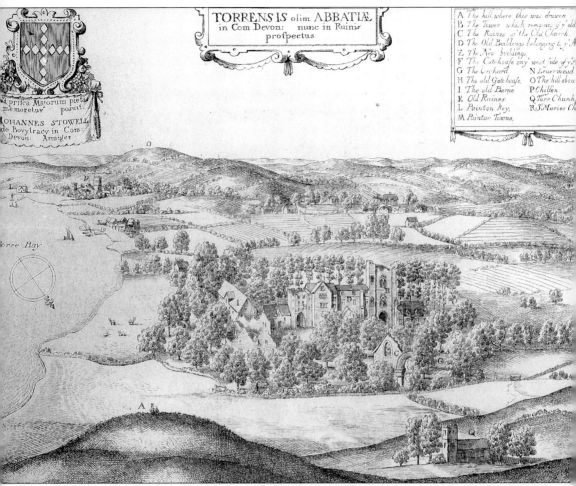

TORRENSIS olim ABBATIÆ
in Com Devon: nunc in Ruinis
prospectus

A The hill where this was drawn
B The Tower which remaines of y.e old
C The Ruines of the Old Church
D The Old Buildings belonging to y.e A
E The New buildings.
F The Gatehouse ony.e west side of y.e
G The Orchard   N Leuermead
H The old Gatehouse. O The hill abou
I The Old Barne   P Chilson
K Old Ruines.   Q Torr Church
L Painton Key.   R S.t Maries Ch
M Painton Towns.

Torre Abbey and its environs, c. 1660. The Saxon settlement of Torre, lying between the villages of St Marychurch and Cockington, passed into Norman hands following the Conquest in 1066. Torre Abbey was founded in 1196 and occupied by the Premonstratensian Order of Canons. The monks are credited with building the first jetty at the harbour of Fleete, which then became known as Tor Key and, later, Tor Quay. Following the dissolution of the monastery in 1539, the area came under the control of new landowners and their descendants. For the next 350 years, the destiny of Torquay was shaped by prominent families whose names are immortalized on the town's streets, buildings and pleasure grounds, names such as: Cary, Mallock, Ridgeway and Palk.

Torre Abbey, 1900. The Ridgeway family occupied the property from 1599 until 1662. The Cary's, who sold it to the Borough in 1930 for £40,000, then purchased it. The cows are grazing on, what is now, the approach to the longest hole on the public 'pitch and putt' course. The present-day pin position is by the trees on the left.

Cockington Forge, c. 1890. The De Cockington family held the picturesque manor from 1130 until 1350. The Cary's purchased it in 1375 but, after backing the Royalists during the Civil War, were forced to relinquish the land by Cromwell in 1654. The Mallock family then managed the property until 1932, when it was purchased by the Borough.

Torquay's oldest cottages, from the top of Penny's Hill. These are thought to date from the fifteenth century. Variously called Beehive or Rose Cottages, it became known as Penny's Cottages, named after John and Peggy Penny who lived there until they both died in 1871. In 1956, Florence Robinson, the ex-wife of the BBC Orchestra leader Eric Robinson, purchased the property. During the summer seasons, she played host to many showbiz personalities. Amongst the stars who stayed at the medieval thatched cottage while appearing at Torquay theatres were: Ronnie Corbett, Kenny Ball, Patrick Cargill, Nerys Hughes, Terry Scott and June Whitfield.

Visitors admire Kent's Cavern in the late 1930s. Traces of Neanderthal dwellings were revealed during a fifteen-year excavation. This commenced in 1865, under the direction of William Pengelly, a founder member of the Torquay Natural History Society. In the background, the work continues under the supervision of Arthur Ogilvie, the curator of the society's museum, who was appointed in 1922.

Fleete Mill, 1793. Few visible traces of the River Fleete remain. Rising in Barton, it flowed through the Upton Valley running along what is now Lymington Road, to Castle Circus, then down Union Street, where it met tidal water beyond a mill near the junction with Fleet Street. The mill, of Saxon origin, was demolished in 1835, a period when the urbanization of such rural settings was rapidly underway.

Union Street, c. 1900. On the right, a coach draws up outside the Union Hotel (which was built on the site of Fleete Mill). One of the millstones used for grinding corn was displayed in the bar, until the hotel was demolished to make way for a branch of International Stores in 1963.

Napoleon Bonaparte became an instant tourist attraction on 24 July 1815 when he arrived in Torbay, aboard the *Bellerophon*, on his way to exile. The Emperor had dismissed the British as 'a nation of shopkeepers' although, ironically, his rise and fall was inadvertently responsible for the influx and prosperity of traders in Torquay. The Channel Fleet was anchored in the Bay during the Napoleonic Wars and the area became popular with officers and their wives. The gentry, unable to travel in Europe until the conflict ceased, found Torquay compared favourably with the Riviera. The 'Little General' was also impressed at his first sight of Torbay, commenting 'Quel bon pays' [What a lovely country].

At the time of Napoleon's enforced visit to the Bay, Torquay had only one hotel, named Poulton's after it's owner. It became known as the Royal in 1833, when Princess Victoria was accommodated. Victoria Parade, opposite the hotel, was also named in honour of this occasion. At Christmas 1838, the business was sold to E. Webb, son of the landlord of the Seven Stars, Totnes.

15

Charter Day, 1 September 1892. This saw the incorporation of the town as a Municipal Borough, superceding the Local Board which had existed since 1850. A striking feature of the celebrations was the floral car prepared by public gardeners, Messrs Dyer and Browning, which took part in a mile-long procession through the town. The Borough was extended in 1900, with the addition of Babbacombe and St Marychurch, controlled by the Carys, and Cockington, which was managed by the Mallocks.

The Corporation wheelwright, J. Carthew, and blacksmith, G. Steer, demonstrated their craft during the procession, riding through the streets on a cart complete with a flaming forge.

Also taking part in the festivities were the two horse-drawn appliances of the Fire Brigade. The service was stationed at Market Street from the 1880s until it moved to Newton Road in October 1957.

The Royal Charter was read at the Strand, from the balcony of the Queen's Hotel. Built in 1828, it became Torquay's second hotel, but only after overcoming objections from the Vicar of Torre. In his opinion 'two hotels in the town would be detrimental to its moral health'.

FLORAL COAT OF ARMS, ABBEY GARDENS. TORQUAY.

'Salus et Felicitas' [Health and Happiness], was the motto selected to accompany the Borough Coat Of Arms, adopted in 1893. This floral replica appeared in the public gardens of Abbey Park, which was opened in 1924.

Freedom of the Borough ceremony, 13 July 1921. The honour was conferred on, from left to right: the 'Hardy of Devon' author, Eden Phillpotts; ex-Mayor, Hugh Cumming; philanthropist, Louisa Cary; former Borough Treasurer, John Glanfield; ex-Mayor, John Rockhey: former Town Clerk, Frederick Hex and absent beneficiary, Charles Moyse, the literary scholar.

Two
Special Events

'Opkins: O yez! O yez! O yez!' by J.C. Dinham.
Torquay town cryer, Charlie Hopkins, announced the eightieth birthday of Queen Victoria on 24 May 1899. It was a celebration that he shared, having been born in London thirty minutes before the monarch herself. Informed of this fact by a Council official, the Palace sent Charlie a £5 note and he celebrated in style. From his home in Pimlico, he reflected on his life, stating 'I have had many kind friends, the greatest, of course, of whom is Her Majesty the Queen, God bless her'.

A. LORIMER,
Proprietor.

CARY ARMS HOTEL,
BABBACOMBE.

In kind Remembrance of the Jubilee Year of ..
Her most Gracious Majesty the Queen.

The Landlord of the "Cary Arms Inn," will supply to his Customers this Summer, a Copy of this Record of the Dates of the Visits to Babbicombe by Members of the Royal Family. .

1ST AUGUST, 1833—The Duchess of Kent, with her daughter the Princess Victoria, landed at Torquay, and after a brief stay at the Royal Hotel, paid a visit to Mrs. Whitehead at Babbicombe.

AUGUST, 1846—The Royal Squadron, with Her most Gracious Majesty the Queen and Prince Albert and others on board, anchored in the Bay.

ON MONDAY, JULY 19TH, 1852—At three o'clock p.m., the Royal Squadron was observed by the preventive men on the heights at Babbicombe steering for Torquay; bearing 20 to 25 miles S.E. The active Coastguards at Babbicombe were immediately numbered in their uniforms, and were soon afloat in a fine boat to do honor to the Royal Standard of England. As soon as the boat was seen by the Squadron, the Royal Yacht altered its course, and soon came within hail. His Royal Highness Prince Albert and his Private Secretary, stepped into the boat and were immediately pulled on shore. The excitement among the inhabitants of the beautiful hamlet of Babbicombe was immense, and they crowded the shore and every part of the hills to give expression to their feelings of loyalty. Mrs. Whitehead received the Royal party as they landed, and Mr. Gasking, the proprietor of the beautiful hotel, the "Cary Arms" which is so picturesquely situated at the foot of the cliff, caused mahogany planks to be laid down to facilitate the passage of the Royal party over the beach.

His Royal Highness walked to the top of the hill, where he engaged a carriage belonging to Henry Manning, coach proprietor of St. Mary Church, requesting to be driven to the principal parts of Torquay. His Royal Highness went through the New Terrace Drive from Torquay by Meadfoot to Babbicombe Hill, where an immense number of persons had assembled to show respect to the Consort of our beloved Queen. Miss Keyse had the honor of conducting the Prince through the celebrated grounds of Mrs. Whitehead, with which his Royal Highness expressed himself highly gratified.

During the time Prince Albert was thus employed, the Prince of Wales and his brother landed with Captain Crispin, and were engaged in examining and enjoying the beauties of Mrs. Whitehead's house and grounds.

At the request of Her Majesty, Lieutenant Shairp, of the Coastguard Service, went on board the Royal Yacht, and was graciously requested to steer the Barge along the coast, the scenery of which was much admired, and sketches were taken of some of the point most interesting. The urbanity of the Royal party was the delight of all who had the pleasure of enjoying an intercourse so unexpected and so novel.

On the Royal party leaving Babbicombe, Mr. Gasking, of the "Cary Arms" had the honor of presenting the Princes with a lithograph view of Babbicombe, taken in 1846, when Her Majesty graciously anchored in the Bay, and the Royal Squadron is seen at anchor.

AUGUST 5TH, 1879—Another visit of His Royal Highness the Prince of Wales, who took tea at the "Cary Arms," accompanied by Lord Charles Beresford and party.

MAY 18TH, 1880—Another visit by their Royal Highnesses, the Prince and Princess of Wales, and two sons, Prince Albert Victor of Wales and Prince George Frederick of Wales, and the Duchess of Sutherland.

The landlord of the Cary Arms proudly produced this souvenir of royal visits to Babbacombe in order to commemorate the Diamond Jubilee of Queen Victoria in 1897. It also records the times that royalty had called on Elizabeth Whitehead and her daughter, Emma Keyse, at their home, The Glen, on Babbacombe Beach.

The Garden Room adjoining The Glen, where Princess Victoria took tea with her former nurse, Elizabeth Whitehead, in August 1833. It was later converted into a beach cafe by the Council but burned down a week after opening for Easter in 1928.

The Glen was demolished in 1904, having gained notoriety as the scene of 'The Babbacombe Murder' in November 1884. Manservant John Lee was found guilty of the brutal killing of his elderly employer, Emma Keyse. Incredibly, he survived three attempts to execute him, because the trapdoor of the gallows mysteriously failed to open. In the background, partially obscured by trees, is the Cary Arms. A barmaid found an old piece of rope by a fishing boat on the beach outside The Glen and sold strands to gullible visitors, claiming it was the noose used on the gallows which immortalized Lee as 'The Man They Could Not Hang'!

Celebration of Queen Victoria's Golden Jubilee, 21 June 1887. A long procession makes it's way down Fleet Street. The building on the right is the Vivian Institute, formerly the Salem Chapel, which was enlarged by public subscription as a permanent memorial of the day's event. This School of Science and Art was founded by Edward Vivian and was later to become the Art School building of South Devon Technical College. Torquay Civic Society awarded the building a coveted blue plaque in 1987, by which time it was the Piazza Wine Bar.

The Royal Salute for Her Majesty's Jubilee. Large crowds gathered early at the Strand. The day's festivities started with a peal of bells at 5am followed by a parade of local dustmen!

Spectators perch perilously above shop hoardings in Union Street to obtain a grandstand view of the Mayoral procession, made in honour of Queen Victoria's Diamond Jubilee, on 22 June 1897.

The parade wends its way down Fleet Street. Babbacombe's Cary Park was dedicated to public use to mark the sixtieth year of Victoria's reign.

This lamp-post was erected on the Strand to commemorate Queen Victoria's Golden Jubilee in 1887. The Mallock Memorial Clock replaced it in 1902 and it was relocated to Torre, at the junction of East Street and South Street, where it stood until a motorist damaged it beyond repair in 1961.

Owner of Cockington and former Torquay MP, Richard Mallock, collapsed and died in 1900 while cycling in Scotland. His friends subscribed to erect a clock tower, dedicated to his memory, on 15 May 1902. The three lamps suspended to illuminate the clock face proved inadequate and were replaced by luminous dials (at his widow's expense) in 1924.

Empire Day, 24 May 1905. 5,000 local schoolchildren assemble at Torquay Recreation Ground and sing 'Grace' before tucking in to refreshments provided by the Council.

Mayor Charles Spragge escorts King George V ashore at Princess Pier on Tuesday 26 July 1910. The monarch had arrived in the Royal Yacht to inspect the combined Atlantic, Mediterranean and Home Fleets in Torbay. The exercise had been due to take place at Penzance, but was hurriedly switched when severe weather hit Cornwall.

Workman pose with the tools of their trade during the construction of Princess Pier, which was named after Princess Louise who laid the foundation stone on 5 May 1890.

Princess Pier during the Review of the Fleet, 1910. A concert pavilion was added to the seaward end of the pier in 1901, which survived until destroyed by fire in 1974, by which time it was known as the Islander Show Bar. In the right foreground is the pavilion of Torquay Bowling Club. They played on this green from 1907 until 1912, when they moved to Belgrave Road.

Ilsham Marine Drive, Torquay's finest vantage point for panoramic views of the Bay, was opened at this ceremony on 1 March 1924. Mayor George Iredale looks on as Sir Henry Maybury, from the Ministry of Transport, cuts the tape held by Borough Engineer Henry Garret.

The official party ride along the road where luxury houses for the rich and famous were developed. Ironically, the one-and-a-half mile long drive, subsequently known as 'Millionaire's Row', was built by unemployed ex-servicemen, to whom Lloyd George had promised 'homes fit for heroes'.

The Prince of Wales arrives at Torquay aboard HMS *Hindustan*, 14 August 1911. The prince had been appointed Midshipman a fortnight earlier. His next visit to Torquay took place ten years later, when Mayor Harry Williams received him at the Town Hall, on 18 May 1921.

A huge crowd gathered in pouring rain outside the Town Hall on 15 December 1936 to hear Mayor Denys Phillips proclaim the accession of a new sovereign, King George VI. The nation was still stunned by the abdication speech of Edward VIII four days earlier, when he had announced that he could not continue 'without the help and support of the woman I love'.

Coronation Day of George VI, 5 May 1937. A day off for the pupils of Upton School, where this youngster plays on the railings. The building, erected in 1871, became a Civil Defence Headquarters during wartime. It was demolished to make way for a new Court House, which opened in April 1960.

Torquay Town Hall, 8 February 1952. Mayor Edward Ely proclaims Elizabeth II queen, following the death of George VI two days earlier.

Houses in Queensway near completion, as Mayor Reeves Taylor officiates at the opening ceremony of the Sherwell housing estate in Coronation year, 2 January 1953. Streets were named in honour of the Elizabethan seadogs, including: Hawkins, Grenville, Drake and Raleigh. The second phase of development commenced in the late 1960s and continued the historical theme, using the names of writers and poets, including: Shakespeare, Wordsworth, Beaumont and Ben Jonson.

Review of the Western Fleet, 28 July 1969. The Queen, escorted by Lord Roborough, Lord Lieutenant of Devon, leads the Royal Family down the steps of Haldon Pier where the Royal Barge waits to return them to *Britannia*.

Three
The War Years

One of de Wet's 'Rough Riders' by J.C. Dinham.
This youngster 'steers' clear of trouble, unlike the South African Christiaan de Wet, whose guerilla band harassed Lord Kitchener's forces during the Boer War. In January 1900, the British were besieged at Mafeking, Kimberly and Ladysmith. From the lattermost, a wounded soldier from Torquay, Lance Corporal Hole, wrote home to his family soon after his battalion, the First Devon Regiment, had suffered heavy casualties. This had happened when they had bravely charged out into the open with fixed bayonets to route a nest of fifty Boer snipers. Hole wrote 'I think that the Boers have got more than they bargained for this time, although they have slaughtered a lot of our men, are just as well armed as we are, and have got some good cattle to run about on. I never thought the Boers were so clever with their guns. I have seen some firing in my time, but this beats all'.

Private
Satterford.   Private
Flood.   Private
Blackmore.   Private
Abrams.   Signaller
Leonard.   Private
Legge.   Private
Milford.   Private
Wreford.

Drummer
Frank Tucker.   Private
Burnett.   Private
Fradd.   Private
Neck.   Private
Crocker.   Private
Bowden.   Private
Brinsey.   Lance-Corporal
Hole.

Private
Pidgeon.   Drummer
Furneaux.   Private
Tucker.   Sergeant
Holwill.   Lance-Corporal
Stanbury.   Private
Lock.   Drummer
Henley.   Regt. Policeman
Paul.

Torquay soldiers with the First Devon Regiment. This photograph appeared in a special supplement to the *Torquay Directory* on 28 February 1900, a week before the regiment were relieved at Ladysmith, following a four month siege. Lance Corporal Hole, on the extreme right, was considered to be 'the champion bone player of India' in 1898.

Officers take the roll call of this unidentified squad of soldiers standing 'at ease' on Ellacombe Green. On 23 December 1914, the First Battalion Royal Dublin Fusiliers caused amusement when they arrived in Torquay from India and marched through the town dressed in pith helmets and tropical khaki. They left for the Front three weeks later. By April 1915, only 40 of the 1,100 men survived, following the slaughter at Gallipoli where soldiers fought like 'lions led by donkeys'.

On 22 June 1915, a party of 300 wounded soldiers arrived, in a motorcade of 100 vehicles, from Exeter to be entertained at Torquay Pavilion where they were greeted by the Mayor, Charles Towell.

After the show, the men were served tea in the cafeteria and later enjoyed a short trip around the Bay on board the pleasure steamer *King Edward*. It can be seen moored at the rear of the Pavilion at a wooden jetty, which was built in 1906 and removed by 1939.

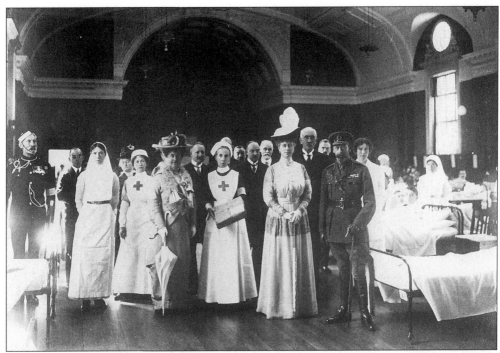

King George V and Queen Mary paid a visit to Torquay on 10 September 1915 to boost the morale of wounded men recuperating at Torquay Town Hall. Budding local author, Agatha Christie, worked here as a dispensary nurse. In her posthumously published autobiography she wrote about her wartime colleagues: 'Most of the ladies of Torquay had never seen a louse, and the shock of finding these vermin was far too much for the older dears'.

An ancillary ward was built to accommodate war casualties alongside the Town Hall, on the site that later became a coach station and is now a car park. In the background are properties on Thurlow Hill.

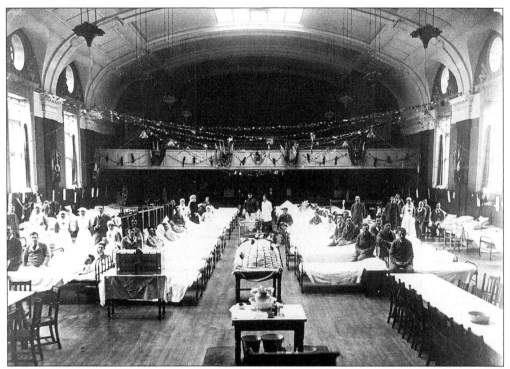

War Hospital, Torquay Town Hall. 'The war will be over by Christmas!' was a popular sentiment in 1914. The reality proved somewhat different and emergency hospitals in the area were doing their best to cheer up wounded soldiers during the Festive Season. Torquay did not forget the men at the Front and sent 2,000 Christmas puddings to Devonians serving in France and Flanders.

British submarines in Torquay Harbour, May 1910. They brought a new dimension to warfare during the conflict. In December 1916, two Brixham trawlers were sunk by German U-boats. *U161*, one of the marauding subs which had caused havoc in the Channel, was exhibited at Haldon Pier in December 1918, a month after Armistice Day.

Wounded Belgium soldiers were treated to an outing on a tram on 26 October 1914, thanks to the generosity of local resident Mr W. H. Oldfield. From August 1917 they convalesced at Herrington, St Luke's Park, the home of former Mayor, William Ball.

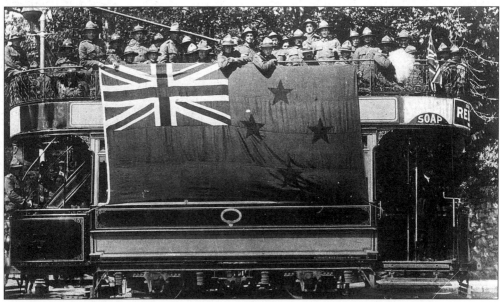

New Zealand troops proudly display their flag before departing for home from Torre Station, 1918. They had recuperated at The Daison and Hampton Court in St Marychurch, and been provided with their own canteen in Torwood Street, called the Kia Toa Club. In honour of six of their fallen comrades buried in Torquay Cemetry, they donated money for a cross of Portland Stone, which was dedicated at St Marychurch parish church on 28 December 1919 by the Reverend Carden.

This war relic was presented to the town on 17 July 1919 'as an acknowledgement of the good work done in connection with War Savings'. The tank stood on Daddy Hole Plain until 1943, when it was melted down for munitions. Its demise must have pleased one local resident, who complained to the editor of the *Torquay Times* soon after its appearance that it was yet 'another interference with the natural beauties of Torquay'.

In the summer of 1939, Britain was gearing up for war. On Sunday 2 July, a National Service Rally was held in Hyde Park before King George VI. Miss King and Mrs Royle, both of whom are sitting in the front row on either side of the Mayor, Charles Price, were chosen, along with the four men in the middle of the back row, Messrs Windeatt, Saunders, Speare, and Hooper, to represent the area in London.

A man carrying a gas mask watches a civilian fire destroy Williams & Cox furniture store on the Strand, 21 September 1939. Three weeks earlier, Britain had declared war on Germany and the local population would soon grow accustomed to such scenes of devastation through enemy air raids.

Torquay's Warden Service was formed in 1937. This marvellous photograph of an unidentified Air Raid Precautions group captures the mood of optimism displayed by ordinary people 'willing to do their bit', confidently prepared to deal with anything that Hitler could throw at them!

This 'Dad's Army' collection of vehicles, requisitioned from local traders for the duration, assembled for 'a show of strength' at a Civil Defence rally held around the perimeter of Torquay Recreation Ground, soon after the outset of war.

On the left of this photograph is Livermead House, where Charles Kingsley resided in 1854 while writing *Wonders of the Shore*. He was not, of course, referring to the barbed wire fence seen running along the seawall to repel would-be-invaders! Opposite the hotel is Corbyn Head, where a six-inch gun battery was positioned. It was never fired in anger, but caused a tragic accident on 11 August 1944, when it misfired at gun practice, killing one regular soldier and five members of the Home Guard.

A large influx of American combat troops were based in Torquay during 1944, prior to the D-Day landings. This group pose for a photograph in Lymington Road.

American troops based in Nissen Huts, erected on what is now Lymington Road Coach station.

The Palace Hotel served as a hospital for RAF officers until October 1942, when the building received a direct hit during a bombing raid which resulted in the deaths of nineteen patients. Earlier in the war, Flight Lieutenant Eric Nicolson had received treatment for injuries suffered on 16 August 1940. Wounded in the eye and foot, he delayed baling out of his blazing Hurricane in order to shoot down a Messerschmitt. A Home Guard sergeant, mistaking him for a German, gave him an extra bullet wound as his parachute landed. The heroic pilot was riding in the Palace lift, when he heard that he had been awarded the Victoria Cross, the only one of the 'few' to be so honoured during the Battle of Britain. 'Nick' recieved a tumultuous reception during a variety show at the Pavilion when introduced to the audience by the Mayor, Charles Price, who later commented, 'I have never met such a modest man in the whole of my long public career'.

On St George's Day 1921, serving MP, Colonel Charles Burn, unveiled a permanent War Memorial in Princess Gardens to honour the 596 men of Torquay who had made the supreme sacrifice for their country. The monument, designed by eminent architect Sir Reginald Blomfield and produced locally by Jenkins Marble Works, was dedicated by the Bishop of Exeter. The sombre ceremony had its lighter moments: a stray black dog wandered to the foot of the memorial and slept throughout the service, until the playing of the National Anthem, when it immediately sat bolt upright, ears pricked, seemingly standing to attention!

Four
Holiday Weather

'Appy 'Garfi' by J.C. Dinham.
'Indian summers' are not uncommon in South Devon, though this gentleman with the sunny smile, who spent the autumn of his life in Torquay, was always cheerful, whatever the weather.

Chapel Hill Meteorological Observatory, c. 1900. Torquay was one of the first resorts to record the hours of sunshine, a practice which proved valuable in the development of tourism. Edward Vivian, Editor of the *Torquay Directory*, collated information at Woodfield, in the Lincombes, from 1846 until 1878. He produced statistics which confirmed Torquay's mild climate and enhanced its reputation as a winter resort, beneficial to people in poor health. Meteorologist, Edwin Glyde, took over from Vivian, recording the weather at Kirkham, Babbacombe (which is now a Medical Practice). From 1888, Alfred Chandler recorded data in the observatory, which was situated near the ruins of St Michael's chapel. The building was abandoned in 1902, when the work was transferred to Princess Pier and Cary Green.

Lymington Road car park, 1951. The postwar boom in tourism resulted in an upsurge of people arriving by coach, a far cheaper alternative to rail travel. Pandemonium ensued at peak periods, with vehicles of all descriptions converging on a single combined entrance and exit.

The Upton Vale Hotel towers over the Lymington Road coach station, which was in use by 1957. Many 'grockles' [a derogatory term applied locally to holidaymakers] did not book accommodation in advance and would knock on the doors of private houses seeking bed and breakfast. Locals obliged though, in keeping with commercial guest houses, 'grocks' were required to be out of their room by 9am and not allowed to return before 6pm!

During the early 1960s, the coach station was still full to overflowing on Saturday mornings during the summer season, with fleets arriving from all over Britain.

Holidaymakers queue for taxis upon arrival. Local children earned pocket money by carrying cases to the taxi rank or escorting tourists to their hotel.

Inner Harbour, winter 1953. Synonymous with the image of Torquay are seagulls, all year round visitors to the resort. They are featured on the Borough Coat of Arms and 'The Gulls' became an obvious choice for the nickname of Torquay United FC.

'Thank Heaven elephants don't fly!' joked a saucy postcard which reflected popular sentiments about being 'splattered' by a seagull. Holidaymakers on Torre Abbey Sands must have been nervous, however, when circus elephants joined them for bathing during a heatwave in 1959!

Ladies Bathing Cove, *c*. 1900. Mixed bathing was not permitted in the resort until 1900. This is the town's oldest recorded bathing facility, dating back to 1810. Later known as Beacon Cove, the beach was closed to the general public from 1977, becoming available only to fee-paying patrons of the ill-fated Coral Island entertainment complex.

The widening of the Central Promenade, 1935. Sun seekers in deckchairs seem undeterred by works carried out at Torre Abbey Sands, while others stroll by for closer inspection. The workmen moved machinery and equipment along rails laid on the beach.

Giant waves crashing over the seawall often results in the Torbay Road being closed to traffic. Cleverly superimposed on this postcard are two Edwardian ladies, who appear to be courting disaster, carrying only their parasols for protection.

The remains of a wooden ornamental toll house at the seaward end of Kings Drive. The building was washed towards the Spanish Barn during the Great Storm of October 1859, when the tide breached the seawall along Torbay Road in several places. Widespread destruction to property was caused during the worst gale ever recorded in Torbay.

The Great Storm of 1938, which occurred in August at the height of the Holiday Season, was not the type of weather promoted in the official tourist guide. Rain definitely ruled out 'play for the day' on Torre Abbey Sands.

A Devon General bus stands abandoned on the Torbay Road, as ladies lift their skirts and make for the safety of higher ground in Abbey Park, during the Great Storm of 1938.

For a single-deck bus, 'ferrying' passengers by Kings Drive in 1938, there was definitely 'No Entry', while ice cream sales definitely 'took a dive'.

A canoe proved to be a practical form of transport when five and a half inches of rain fell in seventeen hours. Many people had to evacuate their homes: some of them were rescued by rowing boat from top-storey windows.

Traffic in Union Street, 1938. Streets resembled rapidly flowing rivers as flood water swept through the town.

These gentlemen look on anxiously as flood water rises outside the GPO in Fleet Street. Telegrams, normally delivered by motorcycle, were somewhat late reaching their destination!

Fleet Street, 1938. Rockheys store employed an engine at the rear of the premises to pump out torrential rain, while staff mopped out by passing buckets along a human chain.

Holidaymakers often seek refuge by shopping during periods of bad weather. A deluge in July 1973 ruled out this option and cars were abandoned in Union Street as a torrent of flood water swept through the town centre. The sign on the corner of Market Street points towards the answer in preventing these scenes. Storm tanks were successfully installed under Ellacombe Green, Fleet Street and Upton Park by 1989.

Police and shocked onlookers at the scene of a tragedy below Babbacombe Downs in 1933. The Mayoress of Torquay, Mrs Denys Thomas, was killed at noon on 19 January, in a car driven by Councillor Coysh.

Madame Thomas was being taken to inspect progress on a beach hut, which was being constructed for her on Oddicombe Beach. The vehicle was descending along the winding road when it skidded on a solid sheet of ice, plunging 150 feet over the steep embankment.

Heavy snowfall is a rare sight in Torquay, though the winter of 1947 proved exceptional in its severity, providing opportunities for snowball fights like this one in Marine Square.

Palm Trees in Princess Gardens experience a culture shock during January 1979.

Ilsham Road, Wellswood. An exceptional gale and blizzard swept the Westcountry in March 1891, causing extensive damage to property. Residents and visitors who braved the elements were required to wear Siberian-like garments. Two dogs in the locality were rescued safely, having spent all night buried in a snowdrift.

A 'Happy Christmas' wish to customers is displayed in this window in Princes Road, now the restaurant area of Dave Hanbury's award-winning fish and chip shop. This occasion was not a white Christmas, although four and a half inches of snow fell on New Year's Eve 1978, which had a sobering effect on revellers trying to enjoy themselves on the coldest night recorded since 1947.

Five
Regattas and Carnivals

'My father's got three little piggies' by J.C. Dinham.
Bringing home the bacon is cheeky chappie Albert John Dymond, a casual farm labourer who was a prominent feature during Regatta time. Singing for anyone who would pay him an ha'penny, the crowd would join in the chorus as he gave stirring renditions of popular songs such as *The Fox is in His Den-O*. A likeable rogue, Albert was well-known to the police and, on one occasion, when sentenced by the Magistrate he allegedly replied: 'Zorry, zur, can't stop got t'cut chaff!'

Torquay Royal Regatta, c. 1898. Crowds gather on Princess Pier to see the festooned vessels in the Outer Harbour. Regattas date from 1911 when a silver cup, to the value of five guineas, was competed for by boats 'not more than twenty-five feet in the keel, and carrying no more then sixty yards of canvas in the mainsail'. The event was granted royal patronage, following the accession of Queen Victoria, in 1837.

Haldon Pier, c. 1898. For landlubbers, the annual Regatta meant one thing – a day at the fair. Here, passengers disembark from the [*Duke* or *Duchess*] *of Devonshire* and make their way to Victoria Parade.

Hancock's Fair, *c.* 1898. All the fun of the fair is taking place on Victoria Parade where, traditionally, coconut shys and stalls were placed opposite the shops. Increasing complaints from traders about the fair having an adverse effect on their business resulted in a change of venue in the 1970s, when it was relocated to Torre Abbey Meadow.

The junction of Vaughan Parade and the Strand, *c.* 1900. Adults and children wait for a turn on the ever-popular Carousel.

Mallock Memorial Clock, *c.* 1912. A tram drops off passengers at the Strand, where the Regatta fair is in full swing.

Regatta fair, *c.* 1952. Larger attractions, including the 'Big Wheel' and 'Helter-skelter' were set up on Beacon Quay. Small boats can be seen on one of the 'hards', built during the Second World War for use by American forces preparing for D-Day.

Babbacombe Regatta has been in existence at least since 1820, with a fair being held, traditionally, on Walls Hill. Here, two boys battle it out in the boxing booth of Hancock's fair, around 1906.

In December 1909, a public meeting decided to 'promote a carnival'. This first event took place on 6 July 1910. King Edward VII had died two months earlier and the carnival coincided with the wedding anniversary of the new monarch, King George V, and his wife, Queen Mary.

Torre Abbey Meadow, 10 August 1932. The annual Torquay Carnival Queen competition.

Miss Betty Parish is crowned 'Queen' by film actress, Joan Marion while the Mayor and Mayoress, Mr and Mrs Frank Callard, look on.

Torquay Fire Brigade follow the band along the Strand in this carnival procession, *c*. 1930.

The first performance of the carnival pageant *Coeur de Lion*, in the grounds of Torre Abbey, 16 July 1935.

Torquay Carnival Concours D'Elegance Rally, 29 August 1933. Competitors line up in their cars along the Torbay Road.

Judging took place at Cockington Court, where Miss Burrows looks on while Miss Mart gives the headlamps a final polish.

Torbay Road, August 1935. From 1920 onwards, the annual event was known as 'Torbay Hospital Carnival' to raise funds for the voluntary hospitals (before the National Health Service was introduced in 1948).

'Miss Exmouth', Enid Franks, is escorted in style, having been crowned, 'Queen of the English Riviera, 1933'.

A 1950s Carnival procession in Cary Parade. The float represents Renwick, Wilton & Dobson, established before the turn of the century as local chimney sweeps, coal merchants and, later, travel agents.

Huge crowds gather to watch the Carnival pass the Pavilion, early 1950s. At this time it was still a concert hall, complete with Municipal Orchestra.

Six
Trains, Boats and Planes

'A fishwife with an up-to-date barrow' by J.C. Dinham.
This lady deserves an honourable mention, alongside those great innovators of modern transport with Torquay connections: Isambard Kingdom Brunel, engineer of the Great Western Railway; William Froude, naval architect and Tommy Sopwith, aviation designer of the Sopwith Camel.

Hollacombe, 21 September 1866. Workmen had not completed the installation of a point and, with no signalling system, the train arriving from Dartmouth ran off Brunel's broad-gauge track.

Hollacombe Tunnel, c. 1900. The railway reached Torre Station in December 1848. Progress beyond this point was hampered due to the financial difficulties faced by South Devon Railway Company (as a result of the failure of Brunel's Atmospheric Engine). There was also fierce debate as to the actual route that should be taken. Torquay Station was established in 1859 and a single-line track to Kingswear, via Hollacombe and Paignton, was finally completed in 1864. The conversion to standard-gauge track was made in 1892.

Considerable delays were inevitable as the single line had to try and cope with two-way traffic. Widening of the tunnel, in order to double the track, commenced in 1908 and took two years to complete.

The soil removed to widen Hollacombe Tunnel was loaded onto goods wagons, transported to Newton Abbot and laid on marshland, where a new goods yard was being built.

GREAT WESTERN RAILWAY

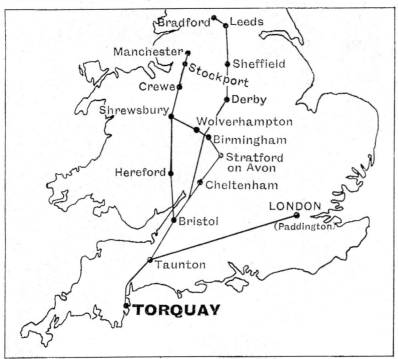

THROUGH SERVICES each WEEK-DAY

between **TORQUAY** and

ALL PLACES shewn on above MAP.

CONVENIENT EXPRESSES from ALL CENTRES of POPULATION.

TOURIST AND EXCURSION TICKETS in the SUMMER. WEEK-END TICKETS ALL THE YEAR ROUND.

Write to the Superintendent of the Line, G.W.R., Paddington Station, London, W.2. for all information respecting travel to TORQUAY.

FELIX J. C. POLE, *General Manager.*

G.W.R. Paddington Station, London, W.2.

This 1926 advertisement for 'God's Wonderful Railway' appeared in the *Torquay Official Guide* which haughtily extolled the virtues of making the journey from the capital, stating 'Torquay is roughly 200 miles from London, but that is not a disadvantage. It ensures that the town cannot be overrun with trippers of a class whose room is preferable to their company. Torquay makes no appeal to the "cheap" tripper'.

Babbacombe Cliff Railway, 1 April 1926. Mayor John Taylor officially declares the line open, at 250 feet above sea level, before making the first trip from Babbacombe Downs to Oddicombe Beach.

The line was constructed on the 2.84 gradient, using 720 feet of track between Babbacombe Downs and Oddicombe Beach. Twelve workmen took fifteen months to complete the dangerous task with no accidents, although the sixteen-stone foreman, Ernest Webster, had a narrow escape when he found himself involuntarily gathering pace as he walked down the steep concrete slope. Luckily, a workmate braced himself against a skip and created a buffer for his runaway boss!

Victoria Parade, 1906. The Sailors Rest was opened on 25 June 1903, by special guest Aggie Weston, who had provided the first temperance missions for sailors on leave in Plymouth and Portsmouth. At these institutions, tea, cakes and religion were available as an alternative to wine, women and drunken brawls.

Men unloading coal, *c.* 1900. Seaborne coal was delivered to the electricity generating station, established at Beacon Quay on 17 March 1898, which operated until July 1924.

The *Torquay* unloading its catch at Fish Quay. In the background is the old frontage of Vaughan Parade, which was rebuilt in 1897.

Landing sprats at Fish Quay in the 1930s. In 1938, Tom Lear, one of the harbour's best known characters, who remembered 'when boats used to sail up George Street', acknowledged that the local industry was in terminal decline by stating that 'where the fishermen used to earn pounds they earn pennies now'.

Unloading an onion boat from Brittany at Beacon Quay, c. 1930. In the background is the Four Hundred Ballroom, now Ritzy's nightclub.

'Johnny Onion', a Breton door-to-door salesman, who cut out the middleman by selling direct to customers in Torquay.

Chelston Cross, later the Manor Hotel, Seaway Lane. Built by eminent naval architect William Froude, in 1867, the house was designed to resemble the interior of a ship. Pioneering research on ship design was carried out here.

William Froude died in 1879. His work was continued for a further forty years by his son, Edmund, seen here with an experimental tank constructed in 1872. Using model ships, hydrodynamic trials were carried out to measure resistance at differing speeds, trims and sea conditions. The same principle was later applied to the aerodynamic design of planes and cars.

The *Duke of Devonshire* operated pleasure trips from 1894 and was joined two years later by a sister ship, the *Duchess of Devonshire* – pictured here departing from Oddicombe Beach.

The *Pioneer*, sister ship of the *King Edward*, at Haldon Pier. Built in 1899 at Fleetwood, she began ferrying holidaymakers from Torquay to Brixham and Paignton in 1906.

The *Princess Elizabeth* paddle steamer operated pleasure trips from Haldon Pier in 1960.

The Western Lady Ferry Service between Torquay and Brixham began in 1946. It was owned by the Edhouse family, who converted four ex-Royal Navy motor launches to undertake the task. One of the vessels made national headlines in 1968, when it ran aground at Elbury Cove. The Torquay lifeboat, *Princess Alexandra of Kent*, was launched and established a record by taking off 122 passengers and a dog during one rescue operation.

Seven years after the Wright brothers had shown that man-made flight was possible, pioneer aviator Claude Graham White upstaged the King's Review of the British Fleet, when he flew over Torbay in July 1910. This souvenir postcard was on sale within days of the event.

The biplane took off from Torre Abbey Meadow and thrilled the crowd assembled on the Torbay Road. The Grant family, owners of the marble works at Watcombe, watched from their carriage parked behind Slade's grocery van.

78

King George V, who had never seen an aeroplane before, watched incredulously from the bridge of the Royal Navy's pride and joy as Graham White swooped overhead, exposing the new battleship's vulnerability to aerial attack. The pilot later confirmed that he could have 'dropped a shell down the *Dreadnought*'s funnel'.

The great attraction of the Torbay Royal Regatta were the giant 'J' class yachts. This amazing action shot was taken onboard 1934 winner *Endeavour*, which later that year challenged, unsuccessfully, for the America's Cup. Straining at the helm is aeroplane manufacturer, Tommy Sopwith, with his wife keeping an eye on the stopwatch.

During the First World War, flying boats were a familiar sight in the Bay as they were housed in specially converted sheds on Beacon Quay. Taking off and landing near Haldon Pier, they were hoisted in and out of the water by crane. Seaplanes also made an appearance in Torquay on 21 September 1926, when the Mayor, Francis Marham, greeted a flotilla that entered the Harbour under the command of Squadron Leader Durston. Sadly, it was only a 'flying visit' as excited spectators in small boats gathered for closer inspection and threatened to accidently damage the aircraft, causing the stay to be curtailed as the visitors returned to their base at Calshot.

The Prince of Wales' arrival at Haldon Moor, 29 May 1930. The Royal visitor was driven through St Marychurch and Babbacombe to the Strand, then through the town to Torbay Hospital on the Newton Road, which had been built two years earlier. From the hospital, the Prince made the short journey to the Shiphay showground, where there were many prizewinning exhibits from his Duchy estates. His Red Ruby bull, Coombeshead Monarch, was adjudged to be champion of its breed.

An aerial view of the Bath & West Show, Shiphay, May 1930. Between Upper Cockington Lane, in the foreground, and Shiphay Manor, on the right, is the show ring, where Sherwell Valley School now stands. The show had taken months of preparation by an army of workmen. Electricity, water and telephones were specially installed. Sheds were erected to accommodate livestock and trade stands provided for the 300 exhibitors. The four-day event attracted over 50,000 visitors.

COME to TORQUAY by AIR
ENGLAND'S RIVIERA

HULL	-	-	TORQUAY	- 3 hrs. 40 mins.
NOTTINGHAM	-		TORQUAY	- 2 ,, 55 ,,
LEICESTER		-	TORQUAY	- 2 ,, 40 ,,
LONDON	-	-	TORQUAY	- 1 ,, 55 ,,
PORTSMOUTH	-		TORQUAY	- 1 ,, 25 ,,
SOUTHAMPTON			TORQUAY	- 1 ,, 15 ,,
BOURNEMOUTH			TORQUAY	- 1 ,, 00 ,,

PROVINCIAL AIRWAYS LIMITED

Door-to-Door

The Fare is **Service**
inclusive

There are **Saves**

Money!

NO Tips
Taxi or
Car Fares
Meals to pay for

HEAD OFFICE :
AIRPORT OF LONDON, CROYDON.
Telephones : Croydon 4117, 4118.   Night, Purley 2859
Springpark 2083.   Telegrams : Provalrway.
SOUTHAMPTON. Atlantic Park Aerodrome.
                                Phone : Eastleigh 109
PLYMOUTH. Airport of Plymouth.
                                Telephone : Crownhill 92
DENBURY. Denbury Aerodrome.   Telephone :
NEWQUAY.   Telephone ; Newquay 225
PENZANCE.   Telephone : Penzance 199
TORQUAY. Messrs. Renwick, Wilton & Dobson, Ltd.
HULL. Airport of Hull, Hedon Aerodrome.
                                Phone : Cent. 32106
GRIMSBY. Waltham Aerodrome. Telephone : Waltham I
NOTTINGHAM. Tollerton Aerodrome.
                                Phone : Plumtree 41
LEICESTER. Airport of Leicester Braunstone Aerodrome.
                                Telephone : Desford 48
BOURNEMOUTH.   Telephone : Christchurch 300.

'Torbay' Airport, some ten miles away at Denbury, was officially opened by Mayor Adrian d'Espiney on Saturday 6 April 1935. The airfield was converted into an army camp during the war and is now the site of Channings Wood Prison.

Seven
Road Transport

Mr Onion: 'Cockles an' Winkles, Vine! Vresh!' by J.C. Dinham.
Anyone who knows his 'onions' will tell you that the transport revolution ushered in the age of the 'horseless carriage' at the turn of the century. The development of the internal combustion engine increasingly challenged the monopoly of the horse and his equine cousins whom, for centuries, had been 'Kings of the Road'. Horseshoes or not, their luck was running out: horsepower was on its 'last legs'.

Union Street, *c.* 1900. At this time it resembled a modern day pedestrian precinct, with only delivery vans amongst the shoppers. Abbott the butcher hangs carcasses in an open window, oblivious to the requirements of basic hygiene, let alone the current problems of BSE and the ban on the selling of meat on the bone.

A cyclist pedals up Union Street before traffic lights, pedestrian crossings, double yellow lines and traffic wardens became necessary to control road users.

Torwood Street, *c.* 1890. Throughout the nineteenth century, road transport depended on horse-drawn vehicles. In the foreground, a well-to-do lady has her own chauffeur. On the right, a cab draws up with a passenger; on the left, deliveries are made to a shop. In the distance, a small trader rides a donkey cart.

Cockington Forge, *c.* 1920. A blacksmith shoes a horse in the days when he served the local farming community. Later, the only horses in the village were to be found at nearby riding stables and the forge became a tourist attraction selling 'lucky horseshoes' to visitors.

A view of Waldon Hill from Rock Walk, *c.* 1875. A lone cabman waits for a fare on the Torbay Road. To the left, beyond Abbey Crescent, is the toll house, which collected money from road users from 1840 until 1862. By 1892, it was being used by the Council's head gardener and came to be named Dyer's Cottage after him.

Trams were in service along the same stretch of road by 1908. The Rolls Royce, like the boats, was added later by the photographer to make the postcard appear more interesting.

The Great Dustpan could have been an appliance for dealing with the 'calling cards' of passing horses in the 1880s. It was, however, a Fleet Street store dealing in a variety of discount goods – a forerunner of the 'cheapjack' traders which, a century later, caused controversy by moving into the revamped Fleet Walk Shopping Centre.

The Strand, *c.* 1905. A passenger boards a horse-drawn bus at the Mallock Memorial. In 1858, an omnibus ferried passengers between the Union Hotel and Torre Station. The first regular service between Torquay and Paignton commenced in 1872.

Cawdles Coaches, c. 1912. These pleasure trips operated from stables in Tor Church Road. Passengers had their photographs taken at the beginning of the journey and prints were ready for viewing by the time they returned.

Cawdles kept pace with the transport revolution, running popular charabanc trips from their Lucius street office after the First World War. The posts on the pavement, in the foreground, were used to support the sun canopies of shops.

In 1920, Cosy Cars became the first local company to be fitted with pneumatic tyres, a great step forward in passenger comfort. Also that year, drivers of charabancs, known as 'the working man's motor car', were warned by the Chief Constable of Devon about the dangers of exceeding the twelve miles per hour speed limit!

Employees of Torquay Co-operative Society prepare for a work's outing, early 1930s. In the background is the Albert Road Labour Exchange, part of the redevelopment area completed in 1984, which opened as the Haldon Centre and was renamed Union Square in 1990.

JOY RIDES FOR TWO

RING UP **891** TORQUAY

TWO-SEATER SUPER-DE-LUXE SIDE CARS FOR HIRE
(With Driver)

MORNING RUNS, 3 hrs., 25 miles   £1 0 0
AFTERNOON RUNS, 1½ hrs., 35 miles   £1 15 0
EVENING RUNS, 2 hrs., 15 miles   £0 12 6

DAY AND NIGHT SERVICE

Theatre, Shopping, and other Short Trips by Mileage 8d. per mile

Each car is fitted with a Post Card Kodak Camera and a Ten Guinea
combined Luncheon and Tea Basket for the free use of Passengers

**THE ONLY PRIVATE HIRE TWO SEATER SIDE CARS
IN THE KINGDOM**

THE 'X' MOTOR CYCLE CO.

55 PARKFIELD ROAD, UPTON, TORQUAY

In the 1920s, an alternative to charabanc rides was provided by the X Motorcycle Company, who placed this advertisement in the *Torquay Times*.

From 1907 to 1934, trams and buses were locked in a fight to the finish to win the exclusive right to provide a public service for passengers. Torquay Council begrudgingly accepted the tramway, considering it a 'common' form of transport, suitable only for 'downmarket' resorts, such as Blackpool. However, with the recent reintroduction of environmentally friendly trams by many towns in Britain, it was no surprise that a consortium won Council backing, in January 1998, to conduct a feasibility study to give Torquay a tramway once again, which would provide a tourist attraction and ease transport problems in the town.

Opposite: The X Motorcycle Company operated from Parkfield Road, later the site of Moore's garage. Out of shot, to the right, was Jenkins Marble Works, founded in 1865, which traded here supplying impressive floors, columns, cladding and furniture to famous buildings, including Paignton's Oldway Mansion, before going into receivership in October 1996.

The first motor bus service began in 1898, but was short-lived. Pictured at the Strand is a steam bus, of the Torquay & District Omnibus Company, which was introduced on 2 November 1903, running to Chelston from the old Town Hall in Abbey Road.

A steam bus at Chelston Terminus, 1913. A fatality occurred in the locality in April 1904, when a youngster, James Young, boarded the bus to collect discarded tickets. He jumped off as the vehicle reversed and fell under the rear wheels.

Torre Station, 1907. Torquay's first tram is unloaded and towed to the depot by a team of horses.

Torquay Tramways Company staff, 1911. This photograph was taken at the depot in Westhill Avenue, which became the home of the Corporation dustcarts after the demise of the tram.

The Strand, 1906. Track-laying began at Torre Station in October 1905, resulting in chaos for other road-users.

Fleet Street, 1906. Work was laboriously slow, carried out by navvies with no mechanical aids. A surface current system was preferred to overhead trolleys, but proved unsafe. Horses were electrocuted when they stepped on live 'studs' and an overhead system was introduced in 1911.

Laying tramlines in Higher Union Street outside Torbay Hospital, which later became the County Court House. Beyond is Upton School, now the site of the Magistrates Court, and St Mary Magdelene church, whose steeple was erected as a memorial to the Duke of Wellington, following his death in November 1852.

Victoria Parade, 4 April 1907. The opening of the new tram service was 'conducted' by Mayor John Smerdon, who took the controls for the first journey to St Marychurch, via Torre Station and Ellacombe.

Pedestrians cross the Newton Road in Torre, behind a tram passing Tom Brown's garage.
Another tram turns left into Upton Road on the route to St Marychurch.

A motorcycle combination waits in Union Street, while a tram negotiates the sharp turn from
Market Street.

A tram travels down Forest Road *en route* from St Marychurch to Torre Station, 1929.

Mayor William Webb takes the controls for the ceremonial run along the extended route from Vaughan Parade to the Grand Hotel, 16 April 1908.

Fleet Street, *c.* 1920. A car overtakes a donkey cart by driving on the tramlines. This could be a risky manoeuvre if a tram was coming the other way. Conflict between the competing modes of transport resulted in number of incidents. One driver was thrown out of his donkey cart when the wheels caught in the tracks, another infuriated a tram driver by refusing to move over and let him pass. One car driver, travelling along Cary Parade, tried to pass a tram on the inside and ended up on the pavement, with his wheel spokes in shreds.

Traffic congestion led to an outcry for a more flexible form of transport. Trolley buses were considered but, after much debate, the trams were eventually replaced by a fleet of twenty-four buses, owned by Devon General. The end of an era came when the tram made its final run on 31 January 1934.

A policeman on point duty at the Strand, 1924. The elm tree was planted in 1880 by Lawrence William Palk, later the third Baron Haldon, and was a notable landmark until it succumbed to the ravages of Dutch elm disease.

The Strand, early 1930s. This shows some of the traffic chaos which sounded the death knell for the tram. Private cars jostle with a tram, a double-decker bus and a charabanc. A cab, from the taxi rank on the left, filters into the traffic.

A stark road safety message for road-users, during works carried out on the Torbay Road in the mid-1930s.

Union Street in the 1930s, when two-way traffic was starting to build up.

Junction of Union Street and Fleet Street, 1954. The shops on the left were demolished and levelled to create a large roundabout for the introduction of a one-way traffic system.

Lower Union Street, 1964. The need for a policeman to direct traffic would soon be over, as plans were in place to abolish two-way traffic. In the background stands the clock tower of the old Town Hall, constructed in 1852. The building also housed the police station and one regular offender was Tom Moxhay, who found ingenious ways to escape from the cells. On one occasion, he broke off the bolts of his cell door with his bedstead, on another, he tunnelled his way into a sewer and emerged at the Harbour!

On Sunday 23 May 1965, a one-way traffic system was introduced in the town centre. The two top pictures show Torhill Road which, thirty years later, reverted back to two-way traffic. On the bottom left, beyond the roundabout, can be seen Abbey Road Congregational church, founded in 1847, which has been the site of Tor Haven retirement flats since 1988.

Eight

Sport and Leisure

Off to the races: 'Tuppence all the way' by J.C. Dinham.
Easter steeplechase meetings were held at Petitor, where many racegoers enjoyed a drinking 'spree' which continued long after the last race. In 1899, the Vicar of Ellacombe, wrote to the editor of the *Torquay Directory*, questioning the 'mob rule' of the 'riff-raff' and asking: 'Are these races, with their appalling drunkeness and obscenities, to continue to disgrace our streets, and to turn them into an immoral pandemonium for two days every time Easter comes around?'

Torquay Recreation Ground. This was initially opened by a private company on 29 September 1888. The first event was a football match between Torquay Athletic and Newton Abbot. Five tennis courts and a cycle track were added a year later. A bowling green was laid in 1894, and it became the home of Torquay Bowling Club, until Wombwell's Menagerie appeared on the ground, allowing an elephant to escape which destroyed the green. The owners of the complex experienced financial difficulties and sold out to the Council in 1902. Torquay Athletic Rugby Club left their ground at Plainmoor, moving to the 'Rec' in 1904, and were joined by Torquay Cricket Club in 1926. The elegant ornamental gates, pictured above, were erected in 1910.

Pennyfarthings line up against one of the latest models, at a cycle race organised by Torbay Bicycle Club. A new racing track at the Recreation Ground was opened by Richard Mallock MP, on 10 June 1889. The *Torquay Directory* reported that the first day of the Whitsun event was poorly attended 'as the weather was less inviting for seeking recreation of any kind out of doors, than it was for sitting at home before a fire; and secondly, if anything at all would have attracted sightseers, surely it was Mr Gladstone's visit to the town'. The second day of competition fared better and apparently 'the grandstand was well occupied'. The roof of the grandstand was torn off during a fierce blizzard in 1891 and a new structure built in 1904.

In May 1898, tennis courts were opened on the site now occupied by the Pavilion. A year later, a bowling green was laid in Princess Gardens. The bandstand in the background was positioned on this spot in 1901, where the Royal Italian band, led by Signor Pellegrini, proved popular. The bandstand was removed in 1960, but beyond it still stands an ornamental fountain (below), presented by Mr Young of the Torbay Hotel (on the left-hand side of both photographs).

Mayor George Iredale officially opens Torre Abbey Park, 20 August 1924.

Abbey Park tennis courts had been completed three years earlier and, in 1924, hosted a Davis Cup match.

National Hunt Racing took place at Petitor from 1864 until Easter 1940, when it was discontinued due to the war and never resumed. The grandstand on the left was destroyed in May 1943, during the same air raid which killed twenty-six children and teachers attending Sunday School at St Marychurch parish church. Petitor has also had a golf course since 1909, which came under council ownership after the First World War when a new course, laid out by James Braid – the designer of Gleneagles – was officially opened in April 1921.

Runners take the water jump at Petitor during the 1936 Easter meeting. A year earlier, a London bookie absconded and left his board behind when the favourite won the last race. He was arrested and served three months in Exeter Prison, having been unable to pay the £15 fine imposed at Torquay Police Court.

Plainmoor, FA Cup Third Round Replay, 12 January 1955. The most memorable match in Torquay United's history. Having held Second Division Leeds United to a 2-2 draw at Elland Road, the Third Division (South) minnows ran out 4-0 winners in front of 11,000 ecstatic home fans. The club's finest ever player, Don Mills, skipper for the day against his former team, capped a great display by scoring the last goal two minutes from time. He is pictured here before the kick off, introducing the club mascot, Haydyn Morgan, to the great Welsh international, John Charles.

International Coronation Regatta, 30 June 1937. The six-metre yacht race, which was won by King Olaf of Norway. A week earlier, the Minister of Labour, Torquay-born Ernest Brown, proved a popular winner when he steered a local boat to victory.

Torre Abbey, 2 August 1948. Torquay Amateur Athletic Club member, Sidney Francis of St Marychurch, holds the Olympic torch aloft before lighting the flame at the opening ceremony of the Olympic Games yachting events.

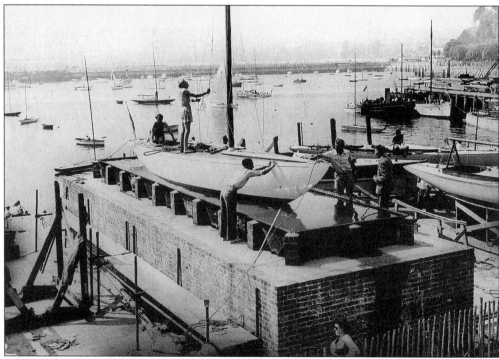

A water tank was built on Beacon Quay, where the yachts of Olympic competitors were measured for size and displacement.

110

The only win for Great Britain occurred in the 'Swallow' class event. David Bond looks on while his fellow crewman, Stewart Morris, receives his gold medal from Sir Ralph Gore, President of the International Yacht Racing Union.

During the closing ceremony of the Games, held at Torre Abbey on 13 August, local girls dressed in white and placed laurel wreaths on the flags of the competing nations, to honour those who had taken part.

The Bath Saloons opened in 1857, becoming known as Marine Spa in the 1930s. Initially a medical baths where invalids could recoup, it became an entertainment complex with the addition of a ballroom in 1924 and a sun lounge in 1929. The National Swimming Championship took place here in 1926.

Marine Spa Ballroom, *c*. 1930. This is the elegant interior where tea was taken while the resident band played background music.

The seaward side of the Marine Spa housed the Royal Torbay Yacht Club, founded in 1863. It received its Royal Warrant in 1875. Torquay Rowing Club, formed in 1869, launched their craft from the slipway under the arches on the right.

The Marine Spa was demolished in 1971 and the Coral Island leisure complex was constructed in its place. Opened by Mayor Sydney Peck, on 29 June 1977, it never matched the popularity of its predecessor and, after a troubled history, closed in 1988. With no other takers, the building became an eyesore and was demolished in January 1998.

The Pavilion opened on 17 August 1912. It was designed by Borough Engineer, Henry Garrett, to provide 'adequate musical and other attractions for visitors to Torquay, especially during the Winter Season'. The exterior has changed little, though the building's uses have ranged from concert hall, theatre, ice-skating rink, to upmarket shopping mall.

Torquay Municipal Orchestra, comprising twenty-five musicians, was augmented for this Wagner Centenary Festival in April 1913. The resident conductor, Basil Hindenberg, diplomatically changed his name to Cameron when war broke out with Germany and, later, received a knighthood for his services to music.

Ernest Goss took over the baton from Basil Cameron as Music Director of the Municipal Orchestra in 1920. The orchestra enhanced its reputation during the 1930s, by regularly broadcasting for the BBC. In 1930, Goss organised the first of a series of Music Festivals, which attracted world-famous guest conductors including: Henry Wood, Adrian Boult and Malcolm Sargent. For many seasons, Mr Goss conducted lavish annual productions of the Torquay Operatic Society and the operatic section of Torbay Operatic and Dramatic Society (TOADS) and was also Chairman of the Torquay Open Air Theatre. The Orchestra was disbanded in 1953 due to financial constraints. Concerts by a small ensemble continued for some years. By 1973, the Pavilion was used for summer shows on weekdays followed by rock concerts on Sundays. The development of pop music brought this comment from Ernest Goss, before he died in 1961: 'Modern music is very clever, but commands admiration rather than love'.

Lionel Digby, one of the town's great postwar characters, was the promoter who brought pop music to Torquay, putting on the town's first rock and roll dance at the Co-op Hall, Union Street, in February 1957. Running his business empire from an office at the 'Old Cop Shop' in Market Street, he started by hiring out local bands to dance halls, then booked chart artists for concerts in Torbay. Among the first acts to appear were: Cliff Richard, Gene Vincent and Adam Faith. In 1962, an up and coming band called the Beatles were turned down for a tour of the West Country, because their manager, Brian Epstein, demanded £150 a night and the astute Lionel was only prepared to offer £100! The soberly dressed impresario is pictured on Oddicombe Beach in 1964. On his left is Screaming Lord Sutch, 'Monster Raving Looney Party' parliamentary candidate. Guitarist Richie Blackmore, on the extreme left, would later find fame with rock band Deep Purple.

The Spanish Barn, Torre Abbey, provides a splendid backdrop for McCarthy's play *If I Were King*, produced in 1952. The open-air theatre was a voluntary venture, aided by the Council, which flourished from 1950 until 1958. In the event of rain, the drama was performed in the Tithe Barn, where prisoners of the Spanish Armada, captured by Francis Drake, had been held in 1588.

Workmen putting the finishing touches to the Regal Cinema, which opened at Castle Circus on 31 July 1933, during the heyday of the silver screen. It was the last purpose-built cinema erected in Torquay, belonging to the same company which owned the Burlington, which showed pictures from 1920 until 1953 at Union Street premises, later occupied by Court's furniture store (until 1990).

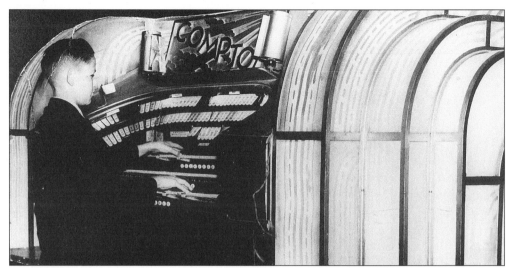

Regal Cinema, 1944. Fourteen year old Raymond Chilvers, billed as 'Torquay's Boy Organist at the Grand Compton Organ', plays for an audience comprising many American servicemen. He had made his debut two years earlier, and continued appearing until called up for National Service in 1948. In 1972, Raymond returned to play a concert for the South West of England Cinema Organ Society with Reginald Porter-Brown, the first resident theatre organist, who had been appointed in 1933. This was the last occasion the organ was played at the cinema. In November 1972, the organ was sold to a private buyer and was later bought by a doctor in East Anglia.

The Regal, owned by Associated British Cinemas, provided Saturday morning matinee shows for children. On 25 October 1975, 'ABC Minors' were entertained by a special appearance of local rock band Tangent. 'Having a go' on the drums is Bryan Holgate, watched on his right by his brother, Alan. Three years later, the cinema became a Bingo Hall and was demolished in 1989. Regal House, the building that rose in its place, attracts queues of a different kind – it's the local Job Centre!

Nine
Torquay Library

Torquay's most popular chairman: 'Any ol' chairs to mend ?' by J.C. Dinham.
This gentlemen's title was in jeopardy when a committee 'chaired' by Ernest Hutchings finalised proposals for the adoption of the Public Libraries Act. It signalled the final 'chapter' in a saga which had taken fifty years to overcome considerable apathy and opposition to providing a free library service for the town.

This souvenir postcard with portraits of the Mayor, John Smerdon, on the left and local MP, Francis Layland-Barratt, on the right, commemorates the opening of Torquay's first public library in 1907. Funds had been provided by American philanthropist Andrew Carnegie, following an approach in 1902 from the Town Clerk, who had expressed 'the hope that this Borough may share in your beneficence'. Joseph Jones was appointed as the first Borough Librarian and the facility opened to the public in October 1907. With 6,970 books, it attracted 3,900 members during the first year. Rapid growth of both stock and membership resulted in a move to larger premises at Lymington Road in 1938. The Carnegie building was then utilized to expand the Town Hall.

The buildings at Castle Circus which were demolished to make way for the Carnegie Library and the new Town Hall.

The laying of the track for the new tramway system is underway in Higher Union Street as Mayor John Smerdon lays the foundation stone for the Carnegie Library, St Valentine's Day, 1906. Copies of current Torquay newspapers and a vellum-embossed copy of the *History of the Library* were placed in a bottle beneath the tablet.

A crowd gathers outside the entrance of the 'free' library at the opening ceremony on 2 October 1907. The building alongside the library, in Higher Union Street, is now a designated 'First Stop' shop of Torbay Borough Council, which was granted local government unitary status in April 1998. The YMCA used the premises from 1920 and they later became an electricity showroom. To the right of the library entrance, below the level of the parapet, is an inscription by local author Eden Phillpotts: 'READ WISELY; FOR A BOOK IS A FAITHFUL FRIEND'.

Francis Layland-Barratt MP, officially opens the new building, accompanied by Mayor John Smerdon. At the ceremony, a telegram from the library's benefactor was read out to the milling throng. The message was 'Best wishes for success of public library and happiness to all your people Carnegie'.

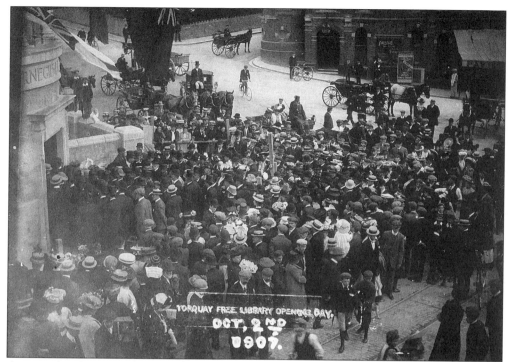

A reverse angle view of the opening ceremony. In the background, to the right of centre, is a building which was the Woods Pavilion Hotel and to the left is the plot where two houses were demolished to build the Regal Cinema in 1933.

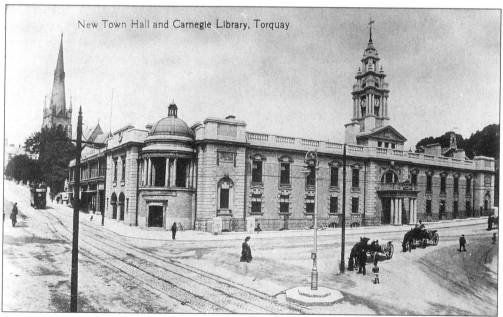

Souvenir postcard of Torquay Town Hall, built alongside the library and opened by Mayor Charles Towell on 30 July 1913.

Carnegie Library in 1938, when business was transferred to a new building in Lymington Road. A tragedy occurred on the balcony above the entrance during the 1920 Peace Carnival: Emma Grant, an elderly guest of the Borough Librarian, Richard Halliday, fell through a glass dome and died of her injuries at Torbay Hospital.

The Torquay Library Staff in 1938, including a uniformed Caretaker (standing on the right) and a Commissionaire (on the left), wearing his campaign medals. Seated in the middle is Richard Halliday. Next to him is his assistant, Eddie Burt, who became Borough Librarian in 1947 when Mr Halliday suddenly collapsed and died while playing snooker at St Marychurch Conservative Club. When books began to inexplicably fly off shelves in a library storage room, it was said to be haunted by the ghost of 'Dickie'!

Chairman of the Library Committee, the Revd Charteris Johnson, placed a commemoration stone for the new building but, sadly, did not survive to attend the official opening on 26 January 1938.

The official party were forced indoors by a heavy rainstorm and conducted the opening ceremony on the balcony of the Lending Department, where the honours were performed by the Mayor of Torquay, Revd Isaac Pugh.

Members of Torquay Library Staff, 1961. From left to right: Wendy Pugh, Barbara Smith, Lorna Smith, Margaret Cox, Laura Chamberlain, Wendy Halbert and Brenda Price. Nine female employees made national headlines in 1966, when strike action was taken for the first time in the history of the British Library Service. The ladies walked out in protest when the Chairman of the Library Committee, Harry Stanway, commented publicly that some of them did not 'give service with a smile'!

The two gentlemen serving behind the counter are librarians from Turkey, who worked at Torquay during a cultural visit organised by the British Council in 1963.

PRINT CLEARLY   Issued | 9/68 | No. 1166

Surname .HILLER...................Mrs. / Mr. / Miss   Resident/Visitor

Christian
Names (in full) .KEITH.................................   Filed at

Home Address .29, PENSFORD AVE...........
.KEW RICHMOND SURREY...............

| BM | PN |
| TQ | GN |

Business Address or School
if resident outside Borough ....

Torbay Address (If visitor) CAP MARTIN BRADDONS HILL
RD. E.. TORQUAY...

I agree to comply with the Byelaws, Rules and Regulations of the Torbay Library
Service.
Date ..11th Sept. 1968... Signed .K.C. Miller.............

No. on Electoral List ....

GUARANTEE OVER (To be signed for person not on list)   Form 5/A

Great Train Robber, Bruce Reynolds, on the run after an audacious escape from prison where he was serving a twenty-year sentence for his part in the so-called 'Crime of the Century', was apprehended in November 1968 at Cap Martin, a rented house in Braddons Road East. Two months earlier he had submitted this application for membership of the Library, using the alias Keith Miller. Reynolds, having managed to persuade a neighbour to sign as guarantor on the reverse of the form which stated that he was 'a person whom Books can be safely entrusted for perusal'. The former escapee's *Autobiography of a Thief* can now be borrowed from the Library where he was temporarily a member.

Acknowledgements

With a few notable exceptions, the photographs in this book were obtained from the wonderful collection in the Local Studies Archive at Torquay Library. I am indebted to the Head of Library Services, Peter Bottrill, for allowing these pictures to be used. Warm thanks also go to Reference Librarian, Anne Howard, for recommending me to the publisher, and to Local History Librarian, Mark Pool and all my colleagues in the 'Ref' for their help and support. For additional photographs and information, which have now been added to the Local Studies Archive, thanks are due to Ray Nickells of the Torbay Postcard Club, Ray Chilvers and Lionel Digby. For readers who wish to learn more about the history of Torquay, the following out-of-print books, invaluable to my research, are available at Torquay Library: Barham, Fisher. *Torbay Transport*, 1979. Dymond, R & White, J.T.. *Torquay Chronology*, 1938. Ellis, Arthur Charles. *Historical Survey of Torquay*, 1930. Pateman, Leslie Lownds. *Pictorial and Historical Survey of Babbacombe & St Marychurch*, 1980. Pike, John. *Torquay, The Place and the People*, 1992. Retallick, Leslie. *Torquay in Old Picture Postcards*, 1982. Russell, Percy. *History of Torquay and the Famous Anchorage of Torbay*, 1960